GLORIA:

A LIFE

Books by Emily Mann Available from TCG

Gloria: A Life

Mrs. Packard

Testimonies: Four Plays
INCLUDES
Annulla: An Autobiography
Still Life
Execution of Justice
Greensboro: A Requiem

GLORIA:

A LIFE

A PLAY BY

EMILY MANN

THEATRE COMMUNICATIONS GROUP   NEW YORK   2019

Gloria: A Life is published by Theatre Communications Group, Inc., 520 Eighth Avenue, 24th Floor, New York, NY 10018-4156

The publication of *Gloria: A Life* by Emily Mann, through TCG's Book Program, is made possible in part by the New York State Council on the Arts with the support of Governor Andrew Cuomo and the New York State Legislature.

TCG books are exclusively distributed to the book trade by Consortium Book Sales and Distribution.

ISBN 978-1-55936-960-2 (paperback)
ISBN 978-1-55936-923-7 (ebook)
A catalog record for this book is available from the Library of Congress.

Book, cover design and composition by Lisa Govan
Front cover design courtesy of MS GLORIA, LLC;
art design by Frank Fraver

First Edition, September 2019

For our mothers,
Sylvia B. Mann
and Ruth Nuneviller Steinem

SPECIAL THANKS TO:

Diane Paulus

Daryl Roth

Kathy Najimy

Amy Richards

Christine Lahti
and the original company of *Gloria: A Life*

Mary McDonnell
and the McCarter cast

Manda Bliss, Anna Morton, Debbie Bisno,
and McCarter Theatre Center

Sammi Cannold
and The American Repertory Theater

André Bishop, Anne Cattaneo,
and Lincoln Center Theater

CONTENTS

FOREWORD

By Gloria Steinem

The play you are about to read has a story of its own.

It begins with Kathy Najimy, actor and activist, telling me that I should turn my life into a one-woman play and that I should be in it. Kathy often helps women tell their stories, and sharing them is what feminism is all about, but the word "play" was beyond me. I've never conquered my fear of public speaking, much less faced it every night and twice on matinee days. Altogether, this idea seemed about as likely as a one-person trip to Mars.

Then Kathy took her idea to Daryl Roth, a woman we both admired for her success in the risky and masculine world of producing plays. Years before, Kathy had directed an Off-Broadway musical Daryl produced, and since then, she had not only produced more Broadway plays, but established two Off-Broadway theaters of her own.

To my serious surprise, Daryl also thought this was a good idea. Not only that, but she brought the project to André Bishop,

Artistic Director of Lincoln Center, and together, they took the first step of commissioning Emily Mann, an award-winning playwright and director, to write the script. Emily had written *Having Our Say*, a play about two elderly sisters living in Harlem, whose kitchen talk over the years somehow embodies the entire civil rights movement. It was a play I loved. Clearly, she understood that our personal lives are part of movements—and vice versa.

Now, three smart women were saying this play was possible. More importantly, they were women I trusted, and nothing but nothing replaces trust.

Though Emily had a busy life as Artistic Director of the McCarter Theatre Center in Princeton, she read, researched, and asked questions. My only job was to answer as honestly as I could, and to conjure up feminists like Flo Kennedy, Bella Abzug and Wilma Mankiller who were ahead of me on an activist path. Because living in the future is an occupational hazard of organizers, this look at the past was new to me. I got help from Kathy and also from my colleague and co-conspirator, Amy Richards, who knows everything or where to find it—she could be the smartest person on earth.

Emily created drafts of scenes and more drafts, then a first script. André Bishop and Daryl arranged a workshop in the basement of Lincoln Center where I and a couple of professional actors would read and do walk-throughs. At the end of a week, a few friends and relatives would be invited to watch and respond.

For me, those days were a revelation. Never having been part of creating a play, I didn't know that what we in the audience experience as spontaneous emotion is planned down to the last light cue. Also as a freelance writer and organizer, I never had to show up at the same time and place every day, much less create magic on demand. I could do talks in groups, but only because they were spontaneous. My respect for actors soared. My belief that I could do this plummeted.

Clearly, I had to tell Daryl Roth. Not only had she brought us all together, and invested in this play, but she had involved

André Bishop, who gave us time and rehearsal space. I've never felt so guilty about anything. I got up the courage to invite them both to lunch.

After listening kindly and patiently to my recital of why I couldn't do this, Daryl said, "I understand, don't worry, someone else can play you."

With those magical words, this play acquired a life of its own.

What I had been dreading turned out to be a turning point I will never forget.

Amy Richards, a creative consultant on this play, had been suggesting Diane Paulus as a director from the beginning. Her communal way of working seemed just right for a movement play. (Go online, watch Diane discuss the "Art of the Rehearsal," and you will see why.) She also was Daryl and Emily's first choice, and despite a packed schedule as Artistic Director of The American Repertory Theater, she said yes.

Christine Lahti, an actor I greatly admired and also someone I knew, agreed to play my role. Emily and Diane also looked for actors to play such larger-than-life figures as Florynce Kennedy, the civil rights lawyer and feminist activist who was my speaking partner; and Bella Abzug, a force of nature and a legendary member of Congress. Some actors were called upon to play more than one role. For instance, one talented woman performed the miracle of becoming both my mother and Bella, two very different people.

To play the late Wilma Mankiller, Principal Chief of the Cherokee Nation—who showed me and so many others that feminism is memory—a young woman named DeLanna Studi showed up. Born in Oklahoma and fluent in Cherokee, she was a cousin of Wilma's, though she had never met this woman she so admired. By embodying Wilma, she felt both she and the audience would come to know Wilma.

At that moment, I think everyone in the play felt the universe was on our side.

Then and now, people ask me about my experience of this play. I explain that the closest analogy was like describing symptoms to a group of wise and kind physicians. I had no idea what the diagnosis might be, but I had faith in it.

My suggestions were more about form than content. As an organizer, I had discovered what a difference it makes to be in a circle—not a hierarchy—and I asked if the audience could surround the stage. Diane Paulus also breaks the invisible wall in the plays she directs. Daryl Roth agreed to reconfigure her theater so that a curved stage area was surrounded by bleachers rising up on all sides, and Diane made the stage friendly with rugs and cushions and piles of books.

Emily knew that I turned lectures into talking circles, and she had the idea of doing this in the theater, too. Act One was the play itself, and Act Two became a talking circle; not a traditional talk-back, but a space for people to tell their own stories and to respond to each other.

Sometimes, Christine Lahti led Act Two, and guest organizers were also invited. I led some, too, and discovered that audiences didn't need much leading. All cast members had to do was simply pass around microphones. People easily spoke about what the play evoked in their lives.

For instance, the script included the story of my abortion, and the kind and courageous doctor who broke the law to help me. This allowed women in the audience to tell their own stories, often for the first time.

One evening, a young black high school teacher talked about his own experience of trying to break down race and gender roles in his classroom. The next week, he brought a dozen of his students so they could see a movement creating change.

At a matinee, an older white man said his idea of playing a masculine role had kept him from being close to his own children. The tears in his eyes said the rest.

Black feminists like Florynce Kennedy and Dorothy Pitman Hughes were in the play, as were images of Shirley Chisholm,

Alice Walker, and others. Yet as was explained in the play, online sources about feminism named only white women. After a few weeks of audience members complaining about this, we heard that those online sources had changed.

Before each performance, a cast member said a few words about the Lenape, the people who lived on Manahatta Island before the British and Dutch arrived. People in the audience talked about how they had and hadn't learned history, and many suggested that, as in Canada, all public events could begin this way.

In this and many ways, a play about a movement became a movement.

For millennia, human beings have been sitting around campfires, telling and listening to each other's stories. Books and computers help us to learn, but only being together with all five senses allows us to empathize, to understand and to act.

This is the magic of both a movement and a play. Like a pebble tossed into a pond, the ripples keep changing lives.

Now, this play and its story belong to you.

—*GS*
New York
August 2019

GLORIA:

A LIFE

Gloria: A Life was commissioned by Lincoln Center Theater by special arrangement with Daryl Roth. It was produced by Daryl Roth, Jenna Segal, Elizabeth Armstrong, Fearless Productions, Sally Horchow, and Alix L. L. Ritchie. It had its world premiere at the Daryl Roth Theatre in New York on October 18, 2018. It was directed by Diane Paulus. The scenic design was by Amy C. Rubin, the costume design was by Jessica Jahn, the lighting design was by Jeanette Oi-Suk Yew, the sound design was by Robert Kaplowitz and Andrea Allmond, the projection design was by Elaine J. McCarthy; the production stage manager was Ana M. Garcia. The cast was:

GLORIA	Christine Lahti
ENSEMBLE	Joanna Glushak, Fedna Jacquet, Francesca Fernandez McKenzie, Patrena Murray, DeLanna Studi, and Liz Wisan

Gloria: A Life was produced by McCarter Theatre Center (Emily Mann, Artistic Director and Resident Playwright; Michael S. Rosenberg, Managing Director) in Princeton, New Jersey, on September 14, 2019. It was restaged for McCarter by Emily Mann based on original direction by Diane Paulus. The scenic design was by Amy C. Rubin, the costume design was by Jessica Jahn, the lighting design was by Jason Lyons, the sound design was by Robert Kaplowitz and Andrea Allmond, the projection design was by Elaine J. McCarthy; the production stage manager was Cheryl Mintz. The cast was:

GLORIA	Mary McDonnell
ENSEMBLE	Gabrielle Beckford, Mierka Girten
	Patrena Murray, Erika Stone,
	Brenda Withers, Eunice Wong

CAST

Seven Women. One performer plays Gloria. All other roles are played by a diverse ensemble of six women. The breakdown in the script is by the first name of the actor who originated each role. Another director may break down the ensemble roles differently. However, Dorothy Pitman Hughes, Flo Kennedy, and Coretta Scott King should be played by actors of color. Wilma Mankiller should be played by a Native American actor.

NOTE

After every performance of this play, there will be audience discussion in the spirit of a talking circle.

A multigenerational, diverse ensemble of actors—six women—help Gloria tell the story.

A bare stage with a few places to sit. Gloria's Persian rugs on the floor. Ideally the play is performed in the round. Projection screens surround the space.

Music of the period underscores the action.

In the original production, both video and live-feed were used, but they are not essential. The script notes where media was utilized. Three cubes, piles of books, a small end table, and a stool were used to create the world of each scene. These set pieces were moved around the playing area by the ensemble.

TIME

When the ensemble and Gloria directly address the audience, we are in the present time. Otherwise, they are reenacting a scene from Gloria's past.

ACT ONE

PART ONE

[Montage: One by one, the screens come alive with images of the Women's Movement, starting with a Seneca woman, Sojourner Truth, Elizabeth Cady Stanton and Susan B. Anthony, Ida B. Wells, to the 1970 March down Fifth Avenue, to Gloria saying: "What we are talking about is a revolution, and not a reform," to the 2017 Women's March on Washington, to present-day protests. The ensemble enters the space and watches with the audience.]

The actress playing Gloria enters the space. The lights change.

GLORIA

(To us) Welcome! Before we begin together, I just want to get this out of the way. Everyone always asks about the aviator glasses. *(Laughs)* I mean, they were prescription, but they were also about protection. The bigger the better. *(Beat)* The hair,

too. But I don't want anything to come between us tonight. *(Takes off her glasses)* Because here's the good news—we're all in this room together and not alone on our computers or cell phones! Human beings are communal animals—we're meant to be sitting around campfires telling our stories—learning from each other. We've been doing it for millennia. In fact, I would say being able to tell your story and listening to each other's stories is the surefire path out, because you realize you're not crazy—the system is crazy—and you're not alone.

Social justice movements start with people sitting in a circle—like this. We called it consciousness raising . . . It's all about sharing what's wrong and what to do about it—and there is so, so much to do—we are in a crisis like I've never known—and it seems to get worse every day. But, I haven't seen such activism as I'm seeing—right now. One hundred and twenty-seven women were sworn in to Congress this year—including the first two Muslim women and the first two Native American women—and one of them is openly gay! Women and people of color are taking back our country. Because of the #MeToo Movement, women are finding the courage to stand up and speak their personal truth more than ever before.

Young people are *mad*—they're just not accepting old divisions of race and gender. They're marching and voting and using the legal system like never before.

You might be wondering why I'm so optimistic, given this shit-storm we're in right now. Well, I am a self-proclaimed hope-aholic. But also, because I know we have made *some* progress.

(Music from commercials of the 1950s.)

[Historical footage of women from the 1950s: women dance around their appliances in shirtwaists and high heels; Father Knows Best clips; women dreamily stroke their washing machines with hypnotized smiles on their faces. Ends with an image: "She'll be happier with a Hoover."]

I grew up with all this nonsense! Who here remembers the fifties and early sixties?

PATRENA

This was a time when there wasn't even the *concept* "equal pay for women."

LIZ

People thought women shouldn't be working at all—white women—because we're taking jobs away from our men and neglecting our children.

FEDNA

While women of color were told—as always!—we have to work—*and* take care of our children (and everybody else's children) —and for low wages.

JOANNA

On a domestic violence call, the cops thought success was getting the victim and the abuser *back together*.

DELANNA

Of course, abortion was criminal—

FRANCESCA

And in Texas, murdering your wife for having an affair was considered—

PATRENA

"Justifiable homicide."

GLORIA

I grew up in working-class Toledo and my biggest dream was—to become a Rockette. Yup. See, I was a tap-dancer as a kid. I think back then entertainment was to girls what sports were to boys—a way to get out and up. I dreamed of dancing my way out of Toledo. I still tap-dance in elevators with muzak—when I'm alone.

[Images of collegiate women of the 1950s.]

(Soft swing music plays underneath.)

I was able to go to Smith College in the fifties and major in Government. I discovered that most of the very bright young women were there—to find husbands. I also noticed that unlike my high school in Toledo, there was not one *(Air quotes)* "Negro" girl in my class. I ask the dean of admissions—a white guy, of course—why:

DEAN OF ADMISSIONS (LIZ)

We have to be very careful about educating Negro girls—because there aren't enough educated Negro men to go around.

GLORIA

(To us) I was so impressed by where I was, that I accepted this racist, sexist bullshit. By the end of senior year, most of the girls are raising their hands in class like this, *(Ensemble demonstrates)* so we can see who's wearing an engagement ring! I assume I'll be wearing one some day, too—I'm just, ya know, putting it off.

When I moved to New York after Smith, I had absolutely no idea what feminism was or that there was any need for a movement. All I knew was I wanted to become a writer—a *political journalist.* I soon found out that the men got all the political assignments, and most women got assigned family, food, and fashion stories.

My high point was writing a long, in-depth article for the *New York Times* . . . on textured stockings!

[Images of Gloria's article: "'Crazy Legs'; or, the Biography of a Fashion."]

The only way for me to write a political story was to write one on spec. It's 1963. President Kennedy has just been assassinated, and Bobby Kennedy is running for the Senate from New York State. I'm covering the campaign, along with:

BELLOW (JOANNA)

The famous novelist, Saul Bellow.

GLORIA

Whom I've just interviewed for a profile, and—

TALESE (DELANNA)

The even more famous social critic, Gay Talese.

GLORIA

We're sharing a taxi.

[Live-feed of taxi scene.]

(Gloria sits between them.)

TALESE

Bobby is so tough to interview.

BELLOW

Yeah, I know. He doesn't talk much.

TALESE

Oh my god, that's an understatement!

(They laugh together, knowingly.)

GLORIA

Well, I've found that the only way to interview Bobby is to bring along somebody who disagrees with him. You can only get good quotes if you bring along somebody he needs to convince.

(A moment. Talese leans over Gloria to Bellow.)

TALESE

You know how every year there's a pretty girl who comes to New York and pretends to be a writer?

BELLOW

Sure.

TALESE

Well . . . Gloria is this year's pretty girl.

(Exit banter:)

Martinis later?

BELLOW

Sure.

GLORIA

(To us) Oh, they probably thought that calling me the pretty girl was a compliment. It wasn't until I got out of the cab that I realized I was mad. And I was mad at myself. Why didn't I say something, get out of the taxi, and slam the door?

[Images of Gloria as a Playboy Bunny.]

I know. Given how much I wanted to be taken seriously and not just be "the pretty girl," you'd think I'd have had more sense than to take an assignment that's haunted my *entire life*.

Even today when I'm being introduced—they'll list my books and credits, of which I'm very proud, and then add:

PATRENA

And . . .

GLORIA

Or . . .

LIZ

But . . .

PATRENA AND LIZ

She was a Playboy Bunny.

GLORIA

So . . . how did it happen? *(Big breath)* I'm a freelance writer, and I go to an editorial meeting at *SHOW* Magazine—

DELANNA

A big glossy arts magazine of the day.

GLORIA

You have to kill a whole tree just for one issue. Okay. *(To editors)* I would like to pitch a story about the books the U.S. Information Service is sending to libraries abroad. It's a tragedy for India and—

EDITOR 1 (FRANCESCA)

(Interrupting) Listen—the Playboy Club is just about to open on East 59th Street.

EDITOR 2 (FEDNA)

The question is whether or not *SHOW* should cover it.

GLORIA

(Impulsively, kidding) Why don't you send Dorothy Parker undercover as a Bunny?

(Everyone laughs.)

EDITOR I

Wait a minute. That's a good idea. You do it.

(The editors exit.)

GLORIA

What? No, no, no! C'mon, I was joking! *(To us)* Well . . . it *is* an assignment, and my rent is due.

(Bunny Mother, in charge of supervising the Bunnies, enters.)

BUNNY MOTHER (PATRENA)

Name?

GLORIA

Marie Ochs. *(To us)* It's my grandmother's name. I don't want to forget who I am.

BUNNY MOTHER

Age?

GLORIA

I'm . . . uh . . .

BUNNY MOTHER

You know the cut-off age is twenty-*five*.

GLORIA

. . . Twenty-four.

BUNNY MOTHER

Twenty-four. Uh-huh. *(Half-smiling, letting her know she knows she's lying)* Occupation?

GLORIA

I'm a secretary. It's boring. I want a more glamourous job.

BUNNY MOTHER

Take it from your Bunny Mother—if you can type, you don't want to work here.

(Bunny Mother exits.)

GLORIA

They're *desperate* for employees so I get hired.

(Wardrobe Woman enters. She starts to dress Gloria in bustier, ears, and Bunny tail.)

And there's nothing glamourous about it, it's like being hung on a meat hook.

(To Wardrobe Woman) Excuse me, this costume's so tight it would give a man a cleavage. It's two inches smaller than any of my measurements everywhere except here. *(Indicating her bust)*

WARDROBE WOMAN (JOANNA)

You gotta have room in there to stuff!

GLORIA

I'm sorry . . . What's that?

WARDROBE WOMAN

A dry cleaner's bag!

GLORIA

Wait a minute. What are you doing?

(She stuffs an entire plastic dry cleaner's bag into Gloria's bustier.)

WARDROBE WOMAN

What does it look like?

Settle down, settle down.

You gotta get three-inch heels. You get demerits you wear 'em any lower.

(The ensemble plays the Bunnies, and the male Bunny Trainer.)

BUNNY TRAINER (LIZ)

All right— It's Bunny training time.

PLAYBOY BUNNY (DELANNA)

At Bunny School, we're programmed on what to say:

(As they do the Bunny Dip:)

PLAYBOY BUNNY (FEDNA)

Please, sir, you are not allowed to touch the Bunnies.

PLAYBOY BUNNY (FRANCESCA)

You must be mistaken, sir—that's your hotel room key, not your membership key.

BUNNY TRAINER

Okay—Bunnies to attention! And here we go.

[Historical footage of Bunny training session:]

(They start to move in a circle.)

We're going to try a low carry! Low carry. Yes! How about a high carry? High carry, yes! And, smile, girls! How about a real high carry? And a bit faster now!

(He starts singing "Reveille."

The Bunnies move faster, carrying their trays, balancing on their high heels.)

Okay. Very good today, girls!! Oh, Marie—in the morning you will be seeing the Playboy doctor for your physical.

GLORIA

(To Bunny Trainer) My physical?

(The women disperse.)

(To us) At eleven A.M., I go to a room in a nearby hotel.

DOCTOR (DELANNA)

(Entering) So you're going to be a Bunny! Just came back from Miami myself. Beautiful club down there. Beautiful Bunnies.

GLORIA

So do you have the coast-to-coast Bunny franchise?

DOCTOR

Do you like Bunnyhood?

GLORIA

It's livelier than being a secretary.

DOCTOR

Okay. This is the part all the girls hate.

(Nurse/Patrena preps the needle.)

You have to have a Wasserman.

GLORIA

What's a Wasserman?

DOCTOR

A test for venereal disease.

GLORIA

That seems a little . . . ominous.

DOCTOR

Don't be silly. All the employees have to do it. You'll know everyone in the club is clean.

GLORIA

(To Doctor) Their being clean doesn't really affect me. And the nurse told me I have to have a gynecological exam. Is an internal exam required to serve food in New York State?

DOCTOR

(Getting impatient) What do you care? It's free and it's for everybody's good. Look, we usually find that girls who object strenuously have some reason . . . (He pauses significantly)

GLORIA

(To us) I let him do the exam.

(The Doctor and Nurse exit. Bunnies enter. Club music.)

Once I'm working, I learn the Bunnies get paid—

BUNNY I (FRANCESCA)

(To Gloria, sotto voce) Like shit. Way less than the ads promised. Also, the club takes half our tips.

BUNNY 2 (FEDNA)

(To Gloria, sotto voce) Yesterday, the manager called me his chocolate Bunny.

GLORIA

(To us) And while they say you aren't expected to entertain the men, I'm constantly propositioned—

(All look to the audience, then:)

ENSEMBLE

We all are.

(Street sounds.)

GLORIA

One night, I leave the club at four A.M. My high heels have destroyed my feet. I must have lost five pounds, probably from sweating buckets from this plastic bag. *(She pulls out the plastic bag)*

I see a woman working the corner.

(DeLanna plays the woman on the corner. They meet eyes.)

She seems more honest than I am.

I decide I've researched enough. The next day, I tell them my mother is sick, I have to quit.

I stay home to write the article.

[Images of the exposé in SHOW *Magazine.]*

"A Bunny's Tale" gets published—and it gives me instant notoriety—plus anonymous threatening phone calls. I also get calls from former Bunnies saying they tried to organize a union and were threatened with acid thrown in their faces.

Fame gave me a voice, but I didn't know how to use it yet. Actually, I didn't try hard enough. I didn't know yet what was possible. Plus—after "A Bunny's Tale," I'm offered assignments like pretending to be a call girl! So I'm grateful when the *New York Times* assigns me a celebrity profile. I interview Mary Lindsay, the mayor's wife—not the mayor of course.

When I deliver my article, the editor gives me a choice:

NEW YORK TIMES EDITOR (PATRENA)

You can discuss this with me in a hotel room this afternoon, *(Almost a wink)* or you can mail my letters on the way out.

GLORIA

Obbbb you! . . . I'll mail your letters.

(To us) I was lucky that mailing his letters didn't cost me my job. Sexual harassment isn't even a term then. It's just called *life*.

My next celebrity assignment is to interview an actor and I have to meet him in the lobby of The Plaza Hotel. He's late, and I'm waiting a really long time. Finally, this assistant manager who's been eyeing me comes over:

ASSISTANT MANAGER (JOANNA)

Excuse me. Unescorted ladies are absolutely not allowed in the lobby.

GLORIA

I'm a reporter, and I'm waiting for one of your guests I'm interviewing—

ASSISTANT MANAGER

Right.

(The Assistant Manager clasps her elbow, escorts her through the lobby, and pushes her out the door, as Gloria protests:)

GLORIA

No, no, wait! *(Straightening herself; to us)* Do I look like a prostitute? Okay . . . I'll wait outside the door. Hopefully, I can see the actor from here. An hour passes—no success. It turns out—the actor *did* come, didn't see me and *left*! His press agent calls my editor.

PRESS AGENT (FRANCESCA)
(Furious) She stood up my client!

GLORIA
The editor misses a deadline—I miss a paycheck I desperately need—and I worry about being permanently demoted to the ghetto of "women's interest" stories.

[Images of the 1969 protest demonstration against the Oak Room at The Plaza.]

However, about a month later, there's a demonstration of women protesting at the same Plaza Hotel because in its fancy Oak Room restaurant—women are not served at lunchtime.

(The ensemble gathers as protesters.)

Okay. I didn't join that demonstration because even though I marched for civil rights and against the Vietnam War, I thought protesting for "just women" was frivolous. But then I read about these women who stood up and said no:

OAK ROOM MAÎTRE D' (LIZ)
Management feels the voices of women disturb men having serious conversations at lunch.

(The ensemble breaks into loud hubbub and approaches the Maître d'.)

[More images of the Oak Room protest.]

You will have to leave. You are blocking the door.

PROTESTER I (DELANNA)
How would you like a sign up there that says "whites only"?

PROTESTER 2 (JOANNA)
We don't want to be intimidated by signs that say "men's buffet."

PROTESTER 3 (PATRENA)
It's the same principle. Women are persons. Women are people.

OAK ROOM MAÎTRE D'
I have no intention of taking the sign down or changing the sign. If you can get a court order to take it down, fine.

PROTESTER 4 (FRANCESCA)
You have no intention of changing your policy of segregated facilities? Is that correct, sir?

OAK ROOM MAÎTRE D'
If you women are hard up for a sandwich, we'll be glad to serve you in the tearoom.

(The ensemble breaks into a cacophony, ends with a woman saying, "I'll show you a tea party!" The ensemble exits.)

GLORIA
Then I get *another* assignment to interview a celebrity who's staying at The Plaza.

(Assistant Manager sees her and comes over.)

ASSISTANT MANAGER
Unescorted ladies are absolutely not allowed . . .

(She wheels on him, enraged.)

GLORIA

(To Assistant Manager) No, no, no! I have every right to be here. Why aren't you throwing out all the "unescorted" men in this lobby, who might be male prostitutes? Or since I know hotel staffs supply call girls to get a cut of their fee—look at me! Maybe you're just worried about losing your commission?!

(The Assistant Manager looks startled, to say the least, turns on his heel, and leaves.)

(To us) I can't believe I just said that. I meet the celebrity, we have the interview, and I write the article with a sense of . . . immense well-being.

And this is how it works—then and now.

We all know women give each other courage when we talk to each other, and listen to each other, and stand up. When one stands up—

LIZ

Another stands up,

PATRENA

And another,

DELANNA

And another . . .

FRANCESCA

And another . . .

FEDNA

And another . . .

JOANNA

And another . . .

GLORIA

And that is exactly what happened when I went to cover my first feminist speak-out. Okay. It's 1969, before Roe v. Wade of course, and there was a hearing in Albany on whether to liberalize New York State laws on abortion.

FEDNA

To testify, the legislators invited fourteen *men*—

PATRENA

And one nun.

GLORIA

You can't make this shit up . . .

LIZ

A member of Redstockings—an early women's liberation group says:

REDSTOCKINGS MEMBER (FEDNA)

How about hearing from women who've actually *had* this experience?!

(The ensemble gathers for the 1969 Redstockings abortion speak-out.)

GLORIA

So they hold a meeting in a church basement in the Village and I go to cover it for my new column in *New York* Magazine— "The City Politic."

[Live-feed video of women delivering testimonies.]

TESTIFIER 1 (DELANNA)

When I had an abortion, I had to pay seven hundred dollars. I went through this cloak-and-dagger business—you know, my boyfriend found some quack willing to stick a hanger up me, and then my boyfriend just . . . he just walks away. We're made into criminals, and the guys just walk away!

(She sits, spent.)

TESTIFIER 2 (FRANCESCA)

When I had it, I thought I was the lowest of the low, that I couldn't get any lower and that I was the worst human being in the world. It wasn't till after my abortion I found out it happened to a lot of other people, too. When I finally told my family—my mother told me *she* had an abortion! And this helped me, knowing I wasn't alone. And I'm sure there are women sitting out here right now who are feeling the exact same thing that I'm feeling.

(Ensemble responds, hubbub.)

TESTIFIER 3 (FEDNA)

(Very upset) I was seventeen when I got pregnant. It was the first time I ever slept with *anyone*. If you don't want the baby—like me—you risk your life—like I did—when I got into a car on 54th and Lexington, and I was blindfolded and taken someplace, I don't know where. I wasn't given an anesthetic; the instruments weren't sterilized; I wound up with an infection—I may never be able to have children! *(She starts to cry)* and this is what women have to go through! Because men want to make women *suffer* for their sins, because it's a sin to get pregnant.

(She sits, spent.
Ensemble gathers around Testifiers.)

GLORIA

(*To us*) I've never, *ever* seen this before—woman after woman standing up and telling her personal truth about something that is one hundred percent a female experience—and everyone here is taking it seriously! So many women need an abortion at some time in their lives, so why is it illegal and dangerous? Why is it a secret and a shame? . . .

But what I didn't say that night—and what I hadn't told *anyone*—was that I also had an abortion.

(*Big breath.*)

Right after college—I'm in London, working as a waitress, waiting for a visa to go to India where I have a fellowship. I'm going partly to escape an engagement to a very nice man I know I shouldn't marry. When I find out I'm pregnant, I'm in a panic. What am I going to do? Throw myself down the stairs? Rent a horse and go galloping through Hyde Park? Drink some Clorox? —All the dumb and desperate things women think of. Then I just happen to go to a party. (*Hubbub*) I meet this insufferable American playwright:

(*British party hubbub; ensemble enters. Gloria speaks to an American Playwright:*)

AMERICAN PLAYWRIGHT (FRANCESCA)
(*Over hubbub, to Gloria*) I couldn't get my play on in New York. Thank God the *London* theater has some goddamn taste—

GLORIA
Uh-huh.

AMERICAN PLAYWRIGHT
(*Over the hubbub, sarcastic*) But now we have to cancel rehearsals because I have to find abortions for two fucking actresses.

(British party hubbub continues, then, they exit as:)

GLORIA

(To us) And that's how I find out that in England if you can find a doctor willing to sign papers saying your pregnancy is life-threatening, you can get a legal abortion.

(She faces Dr. Sharpe, expectant.)

DR. SHARPE (PATRENA)

(After a long pause) I will sign the papers and take this risk if you promise me two things.

GLORIA

Anything.

DR. SHARPE

First, you will not tell anyone my name.

GLORIA

I won't.

DR. SHARPE

Second . . . you will do what you want to do with your life.

(A pause, lets it sink in.)

GLORIA

(To us) I hope you, who knew the law was unjust—won't mind if I say this now publicly, so long after your death—Doctor John Sharpe, thank you. Every doctor who takes this risk deserves our thanks.

(Beat.)

You know, when I wrote my article about the speak-out on abortion—I didn't think to include my story. I accepted I couldn't use the word "I." As a writer, I still had so much to learn about the personal is the political.

My male colleagues at *New York* Magazine—very nice guys—they take me aside:

MALE COLLEAGUE 1 (LIZ)
Gloria, you've worked so hard to be taken seriously.

MALE COLLEAGUE 2 (FEDNA)
You must *not* get involved with these crazy women.

GLORIA
(*To us*) But it's too late—I *am* one of these crazy women. Finally, I understand the radical idea that women are equal human beings. And guess what? I'm thirty-five years old.

You know, the hardest part of waking up is seeing our own complicity in all the humiliations. It's not just that we live in a patriarchy. It's that the patriarchy lives in us, right?

For so many years, I put up with not being able to write the articles I wanted to write; for decades, I put up with daily sexual harassment and condescension; I spent a *lifetime* refusing to trust my own experience. And I believe this experience is a common experience for women—and it's been going on for a very, very long time.

[Image of Gloria with her mother.]

This is my mother, Ruth.

She was a loving, intelligent, terrorized woman.

All I knew growing up is that my mother is someone to worry about, an invalid who lies in bed with her eyes closed, her lips sometimes moving in response to voices only she can hear.

You see, before I was born, she'd had—what was called in those days—a nervous breakdown.

(Mother/Joanna enters, in nightgown and sweater. She takes her medicine in a pool of light.)

She lived in a sanatorium for more than a year. The doctor sent her home with a prescription for sodium pentothal, a pioneer of tranquilizers. It turns out it was the same one given to Virginia Woolf and Sylvia Plath.

She became addicted to what she called "Doc Howard's medicine." She took it for anxiety—but it made her seem drunk—and if she tried to stop, withdrawal led to sleeplessness and hallucinations.

After my sister went off to college, my parents separated. I moved to Toledo with my mother—to take care of her. I was eleven years old. From the age of eleven to seventeen, my mother and I lived in what was once her family house. But when we lived there, it was condemned—rat-infested—and there was no heat.

(Radio music begins.
  Gloria helps her mother into "bed.")

One long Thanksgiving weekend, I'm reading *A Tale of Two Cities* for my eighth grade English class.

MOTHER (JOANNA)
(Waking up) We have to escape! There's a war! There's a war!

(Mother plunges her hand through the window trying to escape. Sound of shattering glass.)

GLORIA
Mom, Mom. Come back to bed. You cut your hand. Shhhhh.

MOTHER
Are there German soldiers outside? . . .

GLORIA

No, no. There aren't any soldiers. There's no war.

(Gloria brings her back to bed, bandages her hand. She holds her mother with one arm as she tries to read her book with the other.)

I bandage her hand and make her take her medicine. When she calms down, I hold on to my mother to keep her from running out into the street, as I try to finish my homework.

(Music shifts from 1940s popular music to classical piano music. Her mother gets up and folds paper.)

I remember once—her taking a piece of paper and folding it into thirds.

You know those skinny notebooks you can hold in one hand? Okay, they didn't exist in her day, so she would take a piece of paper, fold it so you can hold it, and take notes. And she teaches me how to do this. But I had no idea *why*.

It wasn't until I was a grown woman that I found out—long before I was born my mother was a journalist! Like me. She was rebellious enough to struggle out of a working-class family, get admitted to Oberlin, then for years, publish articles, under a man's name of course, and, finally, when she was still in her twenties, she became the Sunday editor of the *Toledo Blade*—which must have been a really, really big deal. I mean, women had barely won the vote!

So—she had a demanding job she loved, a young daughter (my sister), and was married to a kind but gigantically financially irresponsible man—my father—who wasn't supportive of her career. Also, she fell in love with someone at the newspaper—maybe the man she *should have* married—but divorce was . . . unthinkable . . . and she broke down.

(Mother exits.)

She ended up giving up her work, her friends, everything. She followed my father to a lake in rural Michigan where he was pursuing his dream of starting a summer dance resort. No one in my family ever thought my mother should have done anything but follow her husband.

They blamed her for daring to pursue her dream of being a writer—especially after she became a wife and a mother. They thought she brought her mental illness on herself.

What happened to my mother wasn't a personal fault. It was a female fate. And I am determined not to share that fate.

END OF PART ONE

PART TWO

[Montage: 1970, the Fiftieth Anniversary March of a Woman's Right to Vote. Gloria watches.

Historical footage of Howard K. Smith on ABC TV: "Theoretically, August 26th could be an awful day for American males . . . That is the fiftieth anniversary of women's suffrage, and to celebrate it, the Women's Liberation Movement proposes a nation-wide strike."]

(Celebratory music of the 1970s.)

DELANNA

We marched against the war in Vietnam—

LIZ

Arm in arm with the guys!

PATRENA

We marched for civil rights—

JOANNA

And we made the guys sandwiches.

ENSEMBLE

YAY!

FRANCESCA

When we women asked to speak—

LIZ

The guys told us our position in the movement was prone.

FEDNA

Finally, we said *enough*.

GLORIA

And for the first time we marched for *ourselves*—as women.

[Images of the march.]

ENSEMBLE

(Singing) Power, power to the women. It's the women's power.
It's the women's power.

(Spoken) Sisterhood is powerful—we demand equality! Sisterhood is powerful—we demand equality! Sisterhood is powerful—we demand equality!

(Music of the 1970s.)

GLORIA

(To us) It's 1970, and the women's movement is *really* taking off!
But I'm getting incredibly frustrated because I can't get any
articles about it published. A couple of editors tell me:

EDITOR 1 (LIZ)

If we publish your article saying women are equal human beings—

EDITOR 2 (PATRENA)

We'll have to publish one right next to it saying women are *not* equal—in order to be objective.

GLORIA

(To us) You can't make this shit up. I start getting a few invitations to speak on campuses—and I see it's the only other way to get the word out. —Now I love the road. It makes me live in the present like nothing else—except really mutual sex and emergencies. And I have to admit—because of my father— I come by my road habits honestly. He spent most of his life living out of a car. *[Image of Gloria's father]* Until I was eleven, we lived out of a house trailer *[Image of Gloria at the door of her trailer]* and I didn't go to school. I think I learned to read from road signs. Also because my father never had a steady paycheck, he prepared me to live with insecurity—which is great in both movement organizing and freelance writing—and not just live with it, but want it. But there was one small problem. See, I had a near pathological fear of public speaking—I go to a speech teacher.

(To Teacher) I actually lose all my saliva, and each tooth feels like it has a little angora sweater on it.

SPEECH TEACHER (FRANCESCA)

You've been two things—a dancer and a writer, and both mean you don't want to talk.

GLORIA

Good point. *(To us)* So I ask the most fearless women I know to speak with me.

[Image of Dorothy Pitman Hughes.]

This is Dorothy Pitman Hughes. She's way, *way* ahead of her time because she invented—

DOROTHY (FEDNA)
One of the first nonsexist, multiracial childcare centers.

GLORIA
We focus on going mainly to the South—

DOROTHY
Because we see there are feminist speakers going out in other parts of the country—

GLORIA
Less likely in the South, and less likely—

DOROTHY AND GLORIA
The two of us *together* in the South.

(Psychedelic rock music.)

[Image from 1971 of Dorothy Pitman Hughes and Gloria raising fists. Image cross-fades to them in the same pose decades later in 2014.]

GLORIA
Dorothy teaches me by making me speak first, and I discover—I don't die! Actually, I *have* to go first because coming after her is an anti-climax.

DOROTHY
(To the onstage crowd and us) Lots of people can't see moving towards their own freedom, but I am asking you women here

tonight to join me and be loud enough to make change happen everywhere! I believe that if the kitchen isn't good enough for my husband, it isn't good enough for me.

DELANNA

The places are packed and incredibly diverse.

JOANNA

Whether it's a tiny group in a church basement or a rally of a thousand people—

LIZ AND FRANCESCA

The response is overwhelming.

GLORIA

We make a space for women to come together and talk.

DOROTHY

Discussions go on for hours! We give people something to respond to—

GLORIA

Then we learn from listening.

[Image of Gloria, Dorothy, and her baby.]

Once Dorothy has her baby, Angela—

DOROTHY

I named her for Angela Davis—

GLORIA

I hold the baby while she speaks—

DOROTHY

And I nurse the baby while *she* speaks.

(Spirited music.)

[Image of Florynce Kennedy.]

(Flo enters.)

FLO (PATRENA)

(To us) Sweetie, if you're not living on the edge, you're taking up space!

GLORIA

This is the great Florynce Kennedy. Flo calls us:

FLO

Topsy and Little Eva! Ha!

GLORIA

She's a civil rights lawyer.

FLO

Honey, the law is a one-ass-at-a-time proposition, and what you have to do is stop the *wringer*.

GLORIA

So she gives it up and becomes an organizer.

FLO

(Giving a speech to the onstage crowd and us) Some people say they won't work "inside the system"—they're "waiting for the revolution." Well, when the ramparts are open, honey, I'll be there. But until then, I'm going to go right on zapping the business and government delinquents, the jockocrats, the fetus fetishists, and all the other niggerizers any way I can. The biggest sin is sitting on your ass!

GLORIA

We're taking a cab one day in Boston and talking about Flo's book:

FLO

Abortion Rap.

GLORIA

The cabbie, an old Irish lady, turns around to us and says:

CAB DRIVER (JOANNA)

Honey, if men could get pregnant, abortion would be a sacrament!

(Gloria and Flo crack up.)

FLO

(To Cab Driver) Honey, I am going to speak your truth *wherever* I go!

GLORIA

(To us) It ends up on T-shirts . . . people paint it on walls—

FLO

(To us) It's on placards outside the *Vatican*!

[Images of "If men could get pregnant, abortion would be a sacrament!" on buttons, signs, etc.]

GLORIA

One night, we're getting ready for a rally in the South—we're in Alabama—and the journalist in me is obsessing about getting my facts straight.

FLO

(Grabbing Gloria) Honey! If you're lying in a ditch with a truck on ya, ya don't send someone to the library to find out how much it weighs—you just get it the fuck *off*!

GLORIA

(To Flo) I'm so nervous!

FLO

Now just go on! Get on up there!

(Flo pushes Gloria onstage at the rally.)

[Live-feed of the rally.]

GLORIA

Friends and sisters! Good afternoon!

ENSEMBLE

Good afternoon!

GLORIA

A year ago, I wouldn't have had the courage to speak before this audience, but now, thanks to the spirit of equality in the air, and to the work of my more foresighted sisters, I no longer accept society's judgment that my group is second-class.

[Live-feed ends.]

(Applause.)

FLO

(To the crowd) Don't agonize! Organize! Niggerization is the result of oppression. And it doesn't just apply to black people. Old people, poor people, all women can also get niggerized.

There are very few jobs that actually require a penis or a vagina. All other jobs should be open to everybody!

MAN IN CROWD (LIZ)
Hey! You two are lesbians . . . Right?

(Long pause.)

FLO
Depends. Are you my alternative?

(The crowd hoots at the heckler, then disperses. Gloria and Flo are being interviewed on TV.)

[Live-feed of Gloria.]

TV REPORTER (DELANNA)
WBRC here. Can we get a statement please?

FLO
Honey, we're rising up—it's a brand-new day.

TV REPORTER
(Interrupting) We're here to talk about the women's movement, not the civil rights movement.

GLORIA
(Exasperated) But Flo Kennedy is a much more experienced feminist than I am!

FLO
Women have had enough. We're tired of—

TV REPORTER
Miss Steinem, we want to hear from you.

(The TV Reporter pushes Flo.)

FLO

Don't you touch me. Keep your fuckin' ignorant hands off me!

[Live-feed off.]

(They exit. The ensemble addresses us:)

FEDNA

And you wonder why we don't know the impact black women had on the women's movement?

GLORIA

The truth is, I learned feminism from black women.

PATRENA

But if I say "Second Wave Feminism"—how many of you think of these great women?

[Image of each black feminist accompanies their name.]

FEDNA

Dorothy Pitman Hughes,

PATRENA

Flo Kennedy,

FRANCESCA

Pauli Murray,

DELANNA

Aileen Hernandez,

LIZ

Fannie Lou Hamer,

FEDNA

Shirley Chisholm,

JOANNA

Audre Lorde,

PATRENA

Eleanor Holmes Norton,

FEDNA

Margaret Sloan,

FRANCESCA

Barbara Smith,

GLORIA

Alice Walker . . . .and we could go on and on and on.

(Soul music plays.)

[Images of each black feminist accompanied with an iconic quote from each of them.]

*(The ensemble starts to form a consciousness-raising group.
1970s music.)*

It's the height of the movement and women are coming together *everywhere*.

FRANCESCA

In consciousness-raising groups,

FLO

And speak-outs.

LIZ

The ideal group turns out to be about two-thirds women,

DELANNA

And one-third men.

("We need men"—look for two men in the audience, and bring them onstage to join the scene.)

JOANNA

If the group is half women and half men, women worry about the men sitting next to them,

FEDNA

But if women are the majority, they tell the truth—

FRANCESCA

And men hear it—

LIZ

Often for the first time.

WOMAN I (FRANCESCA)

(Stands) How can I stop feeling guilty about asking my husband to help with the housework after we both work all day?

WOMAN 2 (PATRENA)

Well, close your eyes and imagine how you'd divide the house-work if you were living with another woman. Now open your eyes, and don't lower your standards!

WOMAN 3 (JOANNA)

(Quiet, elegant) When my husband, Nathan, leaves his underwear on the floor, I find it quite useful to *nail* it to the floor.

(Hubbub, laughter.)

FEDNA

Okay! Let's give it up for the guys.

(Applause as the men return to their seats.
A church basement. The ensemble shifts positions.
1970s music.)

WOMAN 4 (DELANNA)

(Stands) My daughter was told at school she could be a nurse but not a doctor.

WOMAN 5 (LIZ)

Which school?

WOMAN 3

Who said it?

FEDNA

My son goes to the same school and he was told he could be a veterinarian—not a doctor.

(Ensemble starts to organize—hubbub.)

WOMAN 2

That's racist and sexist.

WOMAN 5

Listen, the woman who lives down the street from me—her husband is beating her—and he's threatening to take the kids if she leaves. Anyone know where they can go tonight?

(Organizing hubbub.)

GLORIA

(To us) What I remember most about these early years is being flooded with the feeling that if I do only this in my life and nothing more, it will be enough. I'd never felt part of any group before. It was heady, exciting, and *naive!* . . . Because we thought if we could just explain what's wrong—

ENSEMBLE AND GLORIA

. . . People would want to fix it!

GLORIA

We hadn't figured out yet that injustice is—and always has been—very profitable.

(Pause.)

And then, the ridicule starts— "You're a bunch of bra burners!"

FRANCESCA

They pick that up from the protest against the Miss America Pageant in Atlantic City—

LIZ

Organized by poet and activist Robin Morgan.

[Montage of women in Atlantic City protesting in 1968.]

(The ensemble brings on a trash can and props. They throw their bras in the trash can.)

DELANNA

Women put aprons,

JOANNA

Bras,

FEDNA

Brooms,

FRANCESCA

Steno pads,

JOANNA

Girdles!

LIZ

And other symbols of oppression—

PATRENA

Into an ash can on the boardwalk—

DELANNA

And threaten to burn them—

JOANNA

But we never do.

FEDNA

Because we couldn't get a fire permit!

FLO

Women have been *way* too law-abiding for *way* too long!

FRANCESCA

The press loves alliteration—so from then on we're:

ENSEMBLE

"Bra burners."

(The women exit.)

GLORIA

As the movement continues to intensify, ridicule turns to hostility.

(She sits opposite John Saywell, the host of The Way It Is *on CBC TV, for an interview.)*

JOHN SAYWELL (JOANNA)

Gloria Steinem, you should know her. Maybe you've read her, she's written for most major magazines. These days she's working for *New York* Magazine. *New York*—not the *New Yorker*. And the work she's doing is causing quite a commotion. She's very good. *(To Gloria)* We'd love to hear your response, Miss Steinem, to some of these comments said about you.

[Image of tape recorder. Gloria listens to audio recording.]

VOICE (LIZ)

(Audio) "What kind of girl is she? She seems like a real bitch." *(Laughter)* "Oh she must be very aggressive and pushy. You know they have these whole preconceived ideas of girls who get to where Gloria is in life, what one has to do."

GLORIA

It makes me sad because of the "bitch" part. I mean, it really gets to me; I guess maybe it's worse than I think. I mean I don't hear those comments, but what I've come to understand lately is that it's not always personal, it's that all women come in for this kind of stuff. If you don't play your role, you know, if you dare to aspire to something, then you get it automatically.

It's taken me until now to understand what to say when someone calls you a bitch: "Thank you."

Listen—hostility is a step forward from ridicule. Hostility means we're taken seriously. And we felt that in the last election, right? Remember "Lock 'er up!" And now, "Send her back!"

(Hard rock music.)

[Montage of Esquire's *"She," a hideous attack on Gloria with cartoons skewering everything she believes in—denigrating, accusatory images.]*

Yes, that article in *Esquire* with all these cartoons made me cry because it's just so wrong and cruel.

[Projection of Newsweek *photo and caption: "Steinem: Easier Than You Think," with photos of some of her boyfriends: Mike Nichols, Stan Pottinger, Rafer Johnson.]*

Oh and that one! Only if you read past the part about the men I was going out with, do you find out that what I said was: "Making a living as a freelance writer was 'easier than you think.'"

Yeah, I'm dismissed by the media. They depict me as never working hard, and only getting somewhere because of my so-called good looks—as if I slept my way to the top—but listen, if women could sleep their way to the top, there would be way more women at the top. Trust me.

(The ensemble gathers in a rally.)

Then one day at a rally, a woman in the crowd says this great thing to me—

WOMAN IN CROWD (LIZ)
(Calling out to her) Honey, it's important for someone who can play the game—and *win the game*—to say: "The game isn't worth *shit!*"

GLORIA
She helps me see—we all have a role to play. Maybe my role is to help break that false stereotype.

FRANCESCA

There is all kinds of false imaging of us. Like we're all anti-sex—

JOANNA

Have no sense of humor,

FEDNA

Too ugly to get a man—

GLORIA

Just like the suffragists, it's a way—then and now—of trying to stop the movement.

JOANNA

Then a whole group of women—Nina Finkelstein,

DELANNA

Letty Cottin Pogrebin,

LIZ

Suzanne Levine,

FEDNA

Pat Carbine,

GLORIA

Joanne Edgar,

FRANCESCA

Mary Peacock,

FLO

Flo Kennedy,

GLORIA

And more! We put our heads together.

(The ensemble gathers.)

FLO

We've been listening to all these women in our talking circles on the road—

FOUNDER 1 (DELANNA)

We know what women want to talk about, what they want to read!

FOUNDER 2 (JOANNA)

And there's not *one* national magazine for women—that's owned and edited by women.

GLORIA

Okay. So . . . What if—we create a magazine to publish what *we* want to write about?

FOUNDER 3 (FRANCESCA)

Right—a magazine for women—with no intention of designing it around "feminine" advertising—

FOUNDER 4 (LIZ)

Like recipes or makeup ads—

FOUNDER 5 (FEDNA)

What if we create a magazine owned, controlled, and devoted to—

FLO

Making revolutions, not just dinner.

GLORIA

We meet in my living room to discuss the name.

(The women shift places and gather in Gloria's "living room.")

FOUNDER 5

What about *Sojourner*, after Sojourner Truth?

FOUNDER 4

Sounds like a travel magazine.

FLO

Sisters?

FOUNDER 1

Sounds religious.

FOUNDER 2

How about *Bimbo*?

FOUNDER 5

Fun, but trouble.

FOUNDER 3

What about *Ms.*?

FOUNDER 1

Ms.?

FOUNDER 3

It's in the dictionary—it's a centuries-old term.

FOUNDER 4

(Looking in the dictionary) "'Ms.'—an abbreviation for mistress— like master—it was also used for children—"

FLO

So it has nothing to do with marital status.

GLORIA

That's it!

FOUNDER 1

Short—good for a logo.

FOUNDER 4

And the exact parallel to "Mr."

[Image of the First Ms. *cover.*

Historical footage of Harry Reasoner on ABC TV: "The first edition of Ms., *described as a new magazine for women, is at hand and it's pretty sad . . . It will last about three issues. I can imagine some stark, anti-sexist editorial meeting trying to decide what to do next. After you got marriage contracts, role exchanging, and the female identity crisis, what do you do? As I said, it's sad. Because not even the most Neanderthal of us like predictability. I suppose to these ladies the most patronizing thing you can say is 'I'm sorry.' But I'm sorry. I'm sorry."]*

GLORIA

"The truth will set you free," but first it will piss you off. Right?

ENSEMBLE

Right.

(Ensemble to us:)

FOUNDER 5

We know it will be economically tough because we're not writing about fashion, beauty, and food—as advertisers demand.

FOUNDER 2

Fortunately, we don't know *how* tough.

FOUNDER 1

We cover-date the January preview issue "Spring."

FOUNDER 4

So it can stay on newsstands for three months without disgracing the movement if it doesn't sell.

FOUNDER 3

We fan out around the country to do free press on talk shows, since we can't afford to advertise—

GLORIA

(To us) But when I'm in L.A., I'm on this TV show, and a woman calls in—

WOMAN CALLING IN (FEDNA)

Hello? We can't find *Ms.* on the newsstands!

GLORIA

I call home in a panic—maybe it hasn't been shipped!—then I discover it has *sold out*—in eight days!

ALL

Eight days!

[Historical footage of Harry Reasoner on ABC TV: "I humbly admit I was wrong when I predicted that Ms. Magazine *would fold after five or fewer issues.* Ms. *has every right to feel proud."]*

(Then: upbeat, celebratory music.)

[Montage: The first seven covers of Ms.—*battered wives, women in revolt, Wonder Woman, "Fed Up!" etc.]*

GLORIA

And the letters!

FOUNDER 2

After the preview issue, twenty thousand letters arrive in our one-room office—and they keep coming by the thousands— issue after issue.

(The ensemble becomes the letter writers:)

LETTER WRITER I (DELANNA)

I am writing this on a day when I could not possibly feel any greater depression, alienation, or isolation. I am writing to you because I have no one, male or female, to talk to who will not try to push, cajole, threaten, even beg me into accepting my "proper" role and "duties" as housewife and mother. I live in an area where marriages thrive not on mutual consideration of each other as equal human beings but on the biblical "man is the head of the house" myth. I am probably the only woman in the county in which I exist (not live) who receives your magazine. It has been literally a lifesaver.

LETTER WRITER 2 (LIZ)

I have been told I am stubborn, selfish, domineering, hate men, and crazy, because I talk about that "women's lib" thing. I have been called unnatural because I don't want any more children. I am the mother of two beautiful daughters whom I have been accused of not loving because I think there is more to life than motherhood alone. Your magazine has given me the strength to go on believing that women were not put on this earth to be the handmaidens of men.

FOUNDER 5

Look at this one! *(Reading)* "I read *Ms.* while in prison. First thing I did was break off with my lover who was also my pimp. Second—I wondered why I got arrested and he didn't. Then when I tried researching my case, I found out there are no law books in women's prisons—only in men's—and I made a formal complaint. Ultimately, I got the books. After getting out on parole, I enrolled in law school—I recently passed the bar, and I thought you'd like to know."

FOUNDER 2

This one was written in crayon in block letters—

LETTER WRITER 3 (FRANCESCA)

I am seven years old. The boys get the big part of the play-ground at recess and we get a corner for playing marbles and dolls. We girls are mad as turnips!

GLORIA

"Turnips!" I hope this girl becomes a writer.

JOANNA

But not everyone is a fan!

[Historical footage of Dan Rather interviewing President Richard Nixon on TV.

Dan Rather: "Some political leaders and some others have taken to not addressing women by Miss or Mrs., but they've gone to the Ms.—M-S. Why not do that with White House letters?"

Nixon: "I guess I'm a little old-fashioned, but I rather prefer the Miss or Mrs."

Cut away from interview to a photo of President Nixon and Sec-retary of State Henry Kissinger. Gloria listens to the audio of their conversation:

Nixon: "He asked a silly goddamn question about 'Ms.,' you know what I mean?"

Kissinger: "Yea."

Nixon: "Mrs. or Miss. For shit's sake, how many people really have read Gloria Steinem and give one shit about that?"

Kissinger: "Yea, yea, yea, yea, yea . . ."]

GLORIA

You might be surprised by that, and I was too! Not until all these tapes came out years later did I have any clue that Nixon was in the Oval Office with Kissinger saying these things. Who knew? What I did know was that I was very proud to be on Nixon's "Enemies List." *Everybody* on that list was very proud.

Because of *Ms.* Magazine, I am the first woman ever invited to speak at the National Press Club in Washington.

(Gloria approaches the "podium.")

The less secure the male, the more he has to prove, the more dangerous a leader. Witness Richard Nixon. There is some opinion that Richard Nixon is the most sexually insecure chief of state since Napoleon.

(Pointedly) Sound familiar?

[Historical footage of John Chancellor on NBC TV: "'Ms.' has now been added to the U.S. government list of acceptable prefixes. 'Ms.,' says the government, is an 'optional female title without marital designation.'"]

You know who we have to thank for *that*?! Congresswoman Bella Abzug.

[Image of Bella Abzug, early 1970s.]

BELLA (JOANNA)

(Shouting) This decade has to be a fifty-fifty decade!

GLORIA

Ah, the glorious Bella! When I first meet Bella Abzug, she really scares the shit out of me.

BELLA

Because of the killing of the spirit and the meaning of American democracy I do impeach the President of the United States Richard Nixon!

GLORIA

She organizes a march against the Vietnam War.

[Image of Bella speaking at the march, 1971.]

ENSEMBLE

(Joining arms with Bella) 1, 2, 3, 4, we don't want your fucking war! 5, 6, 7, 8, we don't want your fucking hate!

GLORIA

We end up in this big auditorium at the State Department. Bella is speaking out about our use of napalm in Vietnam, and she's yelling at Jacob Javits, the liberal Republican senator from New York.

BELLA

You're not gonna challenge that??!!

JACOB JAVITS (LIZ)

I'm saying that this is . . .

BELLA

SENATOR!!!! Are you challenging that?! Stop the war! Sign the peace agreement!

JACOB JAVITS

I'm going to continue to fight against this war in spite of you, Bella!

BELLA

And I'm going to keep letting you speak to me! In spite of you!

GLORIA

I've never seen a woman this outspoken or aggressive in public.
One night, after an organizing meeting, we walk home together
on Lexington Avenue.

BELLA

And a truck driver leans out of his cab!

*(Bella takes Gloria's arm as they walk down the street. Sound of a
truck.)*

TRUCK DRIVER (PATRENA)

Give 'em hell, Bella!

BELLA

You know I will! For you!

*(He honks his horn at her.
They walk, arm in arm.)*

GLORIA

Bella, can I ask you something?

BELLA

Sure.

GLORIA

Do you know Al Goldstein?

BELLA

Who doesn't know Al Goldstein? Even his fellow pornogra-
phers are ashamed of him.

GLORIA

Well, Al is *torturing* us at *Ms.* He's advertising an oral sex service with our office number. And what we hear when we pick up the phone—

MS. MAGAZINE RECEPTIONIST (FEDNA)

Hello. *Ms.* Magazine.

MAN ON PHONE (FRANCESCA)

Do you wanna know how big it is?

BELLA

(Rolls her eyes) Oy. Okay.

GLORIA

And guess what he did on my birthday?!

BELLA

What?

GLORIA

I'm leaving the office— I look up on the newsstand—and there's a display of *Screw*—

BELLA

His magazine? —Yeah, yeah— So?

GLORIA

It's hung open to show the centerfold—a graphic, nude drawing of a woman with *my* face, *my* glasses, and *my* hair!

BELLA

No kidding!

GLORIA

Wait! —Down the side of the page are drawings of penises and testicles—

BELLA

Uccch.

GLORIA

And at the top it says: "Pin the Cock on the Feminist."

BELLA

Uh-huh . . . So what do the lawyers say?

GLORIA

Well, we sent a lawyer's letter, and Al's answer came back today—a box of chocolates with a note that says, "Eat it!"

BELLA

(Chuckles) Okay.

GLORIA

(Very upset) No! No! Don't laugh!! It's a nude centerfold—in full labial detail—and it has my face and my head!

BELLA

And my labia.

(A beat. Gloria cracks up.
Gloria turns to us:)

GLORIA

I never want to live in a world without a Bella Abzug in it. The truth is, she's the woman I wish I'd had as a mother.

BELLA

I'm not old enough to be your mother!

GLORIA

It's impossible to overestimate what we all owe Bella.

BELLA

I introduced the first gay rights legislation, and I was for legalizing abortion and for ratifying the Equal Rights Amendment—

GLORIA

And she created one of the most underestimated events, I think, in this country's history—the National Women's Conference in 1977.

[Image of the National Women's Conference.]

FEDNA

The Houston Women's Conference is nothing less than a constitutional convention for the female half of the country.

BELLA

Well, we weren't at the first one!

GLORIA

And only Bella could pull this off. She gets Congress to fund—

BELLA

With tax money!—

GLORIA

Two years of conferences in every state and territory in the union.

DELANNA

Two thousand delegates are elected and issues are selected to be voted on nationally.

BELLA

And then everyone comes together in Houston. Of course, there's this Phyllis Schlafly—who's been elected by no one— she organizes a counter meeting across town and gets at least an equal amount of press.

[Historical footage of Phyllis Schlafly: "A major goal of their move- ment is to establish the homosexuals and the lesbians as just as respect- able, just as entitled to rights and privileges under our system as husbands and wives. I think this is breeding a new type of social disor- der. I think it is promoting a new type of narcissism and it is an attack on the family as the basic unit of our society."]

PATRENA

But at the National Women's Conference, the majority of the delegates support the Equal Rights Amendment—

LIZ

Abortion rights,

FRANCESCA

And lesbian rights as a feminist issue.

GLORIA

My last-minute duty comes from the women-of-color cau- cuses. They ask me to be a kind of scribe for what's called the Minority Plank. I'm honored to be what they refer to as—

WOMAN OF COLOR (FRANCESCA)

Our token.
We finish writing at the last possible moment.

LIZ

Then a representative of each caucus reads their part of the resolution—

NATIVE WOMAN (DELANNA)

American Indian/Alaskan Native women have a relationship to Earth Mother and the Great Spirit, as well as a heritage based on the sovereignty of Indian peoples. The federal government should guarantee tribal rights, tribal sovereignty, and permanently remove the threat of termination.

ASIAN/PACIFIC-AMERICAN WOMAN (FRANCESCA)

Asian/Pacific-American women are wrongly thought to be part of a "model" minority with few problems. This obscures our vulnerability due to language and cultural barriers, and issues such as sweatshop work conditions with high health hazards.

AFRICAN-AMERICAN WOMAN (PATRENA)

The president and Congress should immediately address the crisis of unemployment which impacts the black community and results in black teenage women having the highest rate of unemployment.

[Historical footage of Latina woman: "Comisión Femenil Mexicana Nacional. Deportation of mothers of American-born children must be stopped, and legislation enacted for parents to remain with their children."
Then: Image of Coretta Scott King.]

GLORIA

In the end, Coretta Scott King comes forward with her body-guard—a stark reminder of past tragedies and present danger.

CORETTA (FEDNA)

Let this message go forth from Houston and spread all over this land. There is a new force, a new understanding, a new sisterhood against all injustice that has been born here. We will not be divided again.

I ask the delegates to accept the entire Minority Women's Plank—by acclamation.

(Cheers and applause. Coretta leads everyone in singing "We Shall Overcome." Tears roll down Gloria's face as the singing continues under:)

BELLA

We are here, at last, to move history forward for women.

GLORIA

And this time, America, we will not be denied.

ENSEMBLE

We will not be denied.

(The ensemble disperses.)

GLORIA

After the closing ceremony, I stand alone on the coliseum floor. Will anybody know what happened here? Will all this work continue?

(Fade to black.)

END OF PART TWO

PART THREE

[Montage: The 1980s.

Historical footage of a Ronald Reagan speech: "Abortion-on-demand now takes the lives of up to one and a half million unborn children a year. Human-life legislation ending this tragedy will some day pass the Congress, and you and I must never rest until it does."]

(1980s music.)

[Images of magazine covers, and celebrities, including campaign posters of Reagan: "Make America Great Again."]

GLORIA

(With irony) Anyone here remember the '80s?

[Montage: Gloria's fiftieth birthday party.]

At least my fiftieth birthday is a great party. Actually it was a benefit. My funeral will also be a benefit! Rosa Parks fills the room just by her presence. Bella Abzug sings.

[Historic footage of Bella singing, "You know Bella, I may seem tough, / Compared to you I'm just a cream puff."]

(Beat.)

But hitting fifty is hard. It's the end of something. So, I treat it with defiance, and decide I'll just keep on doing what I've always done—traveling, organizing, fundraising, lobbying, working for *Ms.*, and generally doing a triage of emergencies all for a movement trying to change the oldest power inequity on the planet.

I'm on the road so often, I don't see my mother much in the last years. Actually, I had detached from her. I think I was still so afraid of turning into her. In college, I was embarrassed by her, mortified that she might show up on Parents' Weekend—like Ophelia—drifting helplessly down the river—

(Pause.)

Then on one of my last visits, she told me a story.

We were in rural Michigan at my father's dance resort. My father always took the car to go buy and sell antiques—in order to support us—and my sister was off at school, leaving my mother alone with me—and I was just a baby. There was no phone—no neighbor within walking distance. The last straw was when the radio broke and suddenly it seemed like an eternity since she'd heard the sound of an adult human voice.

So she bundles me up, takes our dog, Fritzie, thinking she'll walk the four or five miles to the grocery store and talk to some people. She's walking along the empty road with Fritzie running up ahead—when a car comes speeding out of nowhere and hits Fritzie head-on. She screams at the driver, but he never stops. He doesn't turn his head—he never even slows down. Poor Fritzie's broken and bleeding but still alive. So, she sits down in the middle of the road, holding him, determined to stop the next car.

She sits there for hours with me in her arms—and Fritzie's head in her lap—but no car ever comes. It's dark by the time he finally dies. She drags Fritzie over to the side of the road, carries me back home, and washes the blood out of her clothes.

(Gloria's mother enters slowly.)

MOTHER (JOANNA)
(To Gloria) When your father came home, I told him: "From now on, I'm going with you. I won't bother you—I'll just sit in the car—but I can't bear to be alone, ever again."

GLORIA
(To us) After she told me this story, I looked in her brown eyes and for the first time, I saw she was my mother—not just someone to take care of.

(To her mother) Why didn't you ever leave Dad? Why didn't you keep your newspaper job? Why didn't you marry the other man?

MOTHER
(To Gloria) Oh, it didn't matter—I was lucky to have you and your sister. If I'd left, you'd never have been born.

(As her mother drifts offstage:)

GLORIA
(To us) I didn't have the courage to say: "But, Mom, *you* might have been born."

My mother died just before her eighty-second birthday. I wish I could have done more for her, been a better companion to her.

She left me all her books— *(She picks up a book)* this one is about Eleanor Roosevelt. I keep finding all her notes in the margins—and I see now how alike we were, though for so long I denied it.

I think of my mother—of all the Ruths—all the great novelists writing only in their diaries, all the great composers singing only lullabies—what a loss, when the roles outside limit the realities inside. Like so many women, I am living the un-lived life of my mother.

(Beat.)

After she dies, I don't stop for a moment. I just keep on working even harder—and I do yet another interview.

(Gloria joins Larry King for a television interview.)

[Historical footage: Larry King interviews Gloria.]

LARRY KING (FEDNA)
Cleveland, Ohio. Hello.

[Historical audio of woman on the phone: "Hi Gloria. I'm so excited to finally get to talk to you."]

GLORIA
Oh wow.

[Historical audio of woman on the phone: "I have a lot to say and I'll say it really quick. First of all, I really believe that your movement was a total failure and I believe you could admit that wholeheartedly. You are one of the primary causes of the downfall of our beautiful American family and society today. A couple questions—I'd like to know if you're married . . ."]

No, I'm not married.

[Historical audio of woman on the phone: ". . . If you have a husband, if you have children."]

No.

[Historical audio of woman on the phone: "No, you don't? Well, let me tell you—don't ever have children, lady."]

LARRY KING
Your life is worse because Gloria is in existence?

[Historical audio of woman on the phone: "Right. I've suspected for the last fifteen years that Gloria Steinem should rot in hell."]

GLORIA
(Turns to us) Of course, there are always responses like this. Sometimes it hurts—and this time—it really, really does.

(1980s muzak from the radio.)

That night, I check into my hotel room. As usual, the welcome music is unbearably depressing. That's all I *ever* heard in those rooms with my mother in Toledo . . .

(She turns off the music, starts to go back to bed.)

But I put all that behind me. Those years made me strong— a survivor— All I ever wanted was to escape that house, and I have! . . . So why do I still feel like I don't matter? . . .

(She breaks. Wiping away tears:)

—Okay. I always joke: "The *examined* life isn't worth living"! but as un-introspective as I am, I start to see how much I missed not having had a mother or a home.

I go back to my apartment for the first time in two years. Good friends come over.

(The ensemble forms a group of friends in Gloria's apartment.)

FRIEND 1 (JOANNA)

Gloria, you don't eat, you don't sleep.

FRIEND 2 (FEDNA)

You don't take care of yourself.

FRIEND 3 (FRANCESCA)

There's not one thing in your refrigerator.

GLORIA

Ketchup?

FRIEND 4 (PATRENA)

We're unpacking these boxes.

FRIEND 5 (LIZ)

They've been sitting here unopened for thirty years!

GLORIA

Twenty-five tops!

(To us) With the help of my friends and a really good feminist therapist—I finally *stop*—and start to look inside. I see that, as a kid, I always felt invisible. I made myself feel real by being useful. No wonder I was always working, always running, always on the road!

For the first time in my life, I write a personal book—*Revolution from Within: A Book of Self-Esteem* . . . You know how you write what you need?

Uncovering the link to the past makes the pain in the present start to diminish. I now understand that, unlike my mother,

I can leave because I can come home. And I can come home because I am free to leave.

I start to spend time—and then more and more time—in Indian country.

[Image of Wilma Mankiller underscored by Cherokee music.]

WILMA MANKILLER (DELANNA)
(In Cherokee) Tsvg-i-tsv-nv-da os-da ge-so-i.
(Translating) Every day is a good day.

GLORIA

I hope some of you know about Wilma Mankiller, Chief of the Cherokee Nation. In a just country, Wilma would have been president.

People always ask Wilma about her name. If they ask her nicely, Wilma explains:

WILMA

It's a title for someone who guards the village. It used to be Whitemankiller, but my family dropped the white.

GLORIA

If they ask her not nicely, she will say:

WILMA

I earned it.

GLORIA

Until I knew Wilma, I thought there were only two possibilities—equality between males and females is impossible and contrary to human nature. Or—equality may be possible in the future, for the first time. Then Wilma shows me a third way—

(They sit together.)

WILMA

You know that Cherokee and some of the other oldest languages don't have gendered pronouns, right? No he or she. People are people—there's no hierarchy.

GLORIA

No, I didn't know that.

WILMA

Because we're matrilineal, women have control over property, children, and our own bodies. Through the ancient use of herbs, timing and abortifacients, we decide when and whether to get pregnant. We used to call white women "those who die in childbirth."

GLORIA

Oh my god.

WILMA

Our female elders have to be consulted before any decisions are made that affect our community. Because our women had power, Washington called us "the petticoat nation"—they thought it was an insult! (*Laughter*)

GLORIA

Of course.

WILMA

The heart of our governance is the *caucus*—an Algonquin word that means talking circles—it's a consensus among women and men. The paradigm of human organization for us is the *circle*, not the pyramid.

GLORIA

(*To us*) A blinding light goes on in my brain. I never knew there was a paradigm that linked instead of ranked.

WILMA

Actually, the Iroquois Confederacy is the oldest functioning democracy in the world—it's the model for the U.S. Constitution.

GLORIA

(To us) Wait. Everybody knows democracy started in Ancient Greece! Right? Then I research the Constitutional Convention and discover that Benjamin Franklin did use the Iroquois Confederacy as his model—

WILMA

How Native nations across America convene to make mutual decisions—

GLORIA

. . . And also allow local autonomy for the tribes.

WILMA

Yes! Franklin hopes the U.S. Constitution will do the same for the thirteen states. That's why he invites two Iroquois men to Philadelphia as advisers.

GLORIA

(To us) Guess what their first question is said to be—

GLORIA AND WILMA

"Where are the women?"

(New beat. Big breath.)

GLORIA

A big part of our problem in this country is simple ignorance of what the oldest cultures have to teach us.

(Wilma comes over to Gloria and gives her the beaded necklace she is wearing.)

This will keep you safe.

[Image of Gloria and Wilma.]

GLORIA

Though she is younger than I am, Wilma becomes my mentor. Her gift for helping people find confidence in themselves is exactly what I need both in my work and in my life. I experience firsthand from her the Native belief that—

WILMA

Wealth is not what you accumulate—it's what you give.

GLORIA

I'm now living with a new understanding. Plus for the first time, I'm free and un-partnered—I finally stopped being a romance junkie! Even though I always loved that quote: "A woman without a man is like a fish without a bicycle," I always had a man in my life—in high school I had two! But to my credit, I never married any of them—so David Bale coming into my life when I'm sixty-six is quite a surprise for me.

[Images of David Bale and Gloria in 2000 and 2001.]

David is the most intensely living-in-the-present person I've ever met in my life—he carries pet food and water around with him, because if he sees an injured dog or cat or bird on the side of the road, he stops to take care of them.

He was born in South Africa and we're looking at all the ways he can get a new visa but there isn't any way except—marriage!—and we want to be together. *The last thing I ever thought I would do in my* life *was get married!* When people used to ask me why I wasn't married I'd say, "Because I can't mate in cap-

tivity!" But marriage isn't what it was when I was avoiding it in
my youth.

(She turns to the ensemble.)

FRANCESCA

We worked thirty years to change the laws.

FEDNA

Back then, if you got married, you lost your legal domicile,

JOANNA

Your credit rating,

PATRENA

Your name,

LIZ

And many of your basic civil rights.

GLORIA

But now, if it gets him a green card and keeps him in the country—why not?

We're together only three years.

[Image: Gloria and David.]

He begins to have memory problems and coordination problems and then he gets really sick . . .

He died of brain lymphoma.

As devastating as his death is, it was . . . a kind of healing.
I got to take care of David the way I couldn't ever take care of
my mother . . .

After he died, Wilma shares something with me.

(Cherokee music.)

WILMA

I had a near-death experience—a head-on car collision on a country road. I want you to know—it was ecstasy. I had a feeling of warmth, of safety. I was flying faster than any human being could fly, looking down at Earth, feeling an immense sense of happiness—as if I was finally seeing the purpose of life!

I wanted to keep flying into this ecstasy, but I pulled back because I thought: My daughters need me.

GLORIA

I keep hoping that David felt that ecstasy.

(She gets up. Beat. Shift.)

Age is supposed to create more serenity, calm, and detachment from the world, right? Well, I'm finding just the reverse. I'm enjoying being a nothing-to-lose, take-no-shit older woman. The older I get, the more I'm living an intensified life, the more likely I am to feel rage when people are rendered invisible; the more able I am to use my own voice, to know what I feel and to say what I think. I'm becoming more radical with age.

JOANNA

Most of us become more radical with age!

GLORIA

I used to think that continuing my active sex life was the height of radicalism. But why not take advantage of hormonal changes to clear my mind, sharpen my senses, and free whole areas of my brain?

JOANNA

Aging gives us permission to be whoever we are . . .

> GLORIA

And say whatever the hell we think!

[Live-feed of Gloria.]

(An interview on guns:)

> GUN VIOLENCE INTERVIEWER (LIZ)

Ms. Steinem, do you have any thoughts today about—

> GLORIA

America's obsession with guns?

> GUN VIOLENCE INTERVIEWER

Yes.

> GLORIA

Well, when you look at school shootings and the concert shootings and the theater shootings and mass shootings of all kinds, what do you see? They're almost always committed by . . . .

(Gestures to Interviewer to answer.)

> GUN VIOLENCE INTERVIEWER

Oh. Uh . . . Men—

> GLORIA

Specifically white men, right? Usually domestic abusers—or sons of domestic abusers—and not poor.

> GUN VIOLENCE INTERVIEWER

Right . . .

> GLORIA

Exactly the group of people told by society they have the right to dominate others. And when they're not able to dominate others, then they kill in order to prove their power. But it's rarely blamed on white men or guns, right?

GUN VIOLENCE INTERVIEWER

Right.

GLORIA

It's blamed on . . .

GUN VIOLENCE INTERVIEWER

. . . Mental health issues.

GLORIA

So what are people saying? That masculinity is a mental disease?

GUN VIOLENCE INTERVIEWER

Ha!

GLORIA

The problem isn't men—it's the "masculine" role that makes some men feel they need to dominate. If we can liberate men from that prison, there's hope for us all. But we can't keep putting movements in silos! You can't put racism over here and sexism over here and gun violence over here! They're all connected.

[Live-feed ends.]

(Planned Parenthood, Memphis, 2016.)

PLANNED PARENTHOOD REPRESENTATIVE (FEDNA)
(Introducing Gloria) At a time when abortion clinics are closing all over the country and violence against women is at its peak, we at Planned Parenthood are grateful to have Gloria Steinem with us here in Memphis today—

GLORIA

Opposing women's rights to control our own bodies is always the first step in every authoritarian regime. In this country right now, white nationalists are going crazy because the white birth rate has fallen below replacement level. It doesn't surprise me that the most virulent anti-abortion measures are coming from Alabama and other southern states because racism and sexism are always intertwined. You can't perpetuate racism without controlling women and reproduction. Keep in mind—the laws governing enslaved people in this country were adapted from the laws governing wives . . . We were all property.

From Nazi Germany to Alabama—from the Vatican to the Taliban—controlling reproduction is the whole patriarchal ball game. Bottom line. Ground zero.

We are not going to be a majority white country, in another like two minutes. And those people who have placed their identity with the white race and the male gender, or both, are in a form of panic and they are lashing out. There's always a backlash. What's so different about this moment is—the backlash is in the White House!

[Historical footage of the Women's March, Washington, D.C., 2017.]

(The ensemble gathers at the march, carrying signs.)

NBC COMMENTATOR (LIZ)

The day after the inauguration of Donald Trump thousands of women descend on Washington, turning the National Mall into a sea of pink hats and homemade signs in support of gender and racial equality.

[Images of America Ferrara speaking to the crowd.]

AMERICA FERRARA (FRANCESCA)

(To the crowd) We march today for the moral core of this nation—against which our new president is waging war—

[Images of marches worldwide.]

NBC COMMENTATOR

Six hundred and seventy cities across the world are having what are being called sister marches—over seven million people have come out to march worldwide.

[Images of Gloria at the march.]

GLORIA

(To the crowd) This is an outpouring of energy and true democracy like I have never seen in my very long life. Sometimes we must put our bodies where our beliefs are. Sometimes pressing send is not enough. The Constitution does not begin with "I, the president." It begins with "We, the people." In his inaugural address yesterday the president said he was *with* the people. Indeed, he *was* the people. To paraphrase a famous quote, I just have to say—"I have met the people, and you, sir, are not the people." We are the people. Don't try to divide us. We are here and we are around the world and we will not be quiet—we will not be controlled. We are at one with each other, and we're never turning back.

(Cheers. Gloria goes into the crowd.)

[Historical footage of the new and young activists: Naomi Wadler, Black Lives Matter, young immigration activists, Parkland students, Janet Mock, Emma González, the women in the elevator with Senator Jeff Flake, handmaids at the Supreme Court . . .]

(To us) The rage many of us are feeling right now can be an energy cell. Whether you're talking to family, or marching with friends, or putting your foot in an elevator door and forcing a senator to listen—don't worry about what you *should* do, just do whatever you *can* do.

All of our stories matter. Each of us here knows things no one else knows, and every one of our stories is of value. So for the very angering and long and exciting future, don't look up—that's giving up your power—look out—at each other, and find shared power.

Dear Friends and Sisters: All my life, I've searched for a family and I found it in the women's movement, my chosen family . . . I know I won't be with you on this earth much longer—though I plan to live to be a hundred. I have to, just to meet my deadlines! I love it here so much I never want it to end. I want the work to go on and on and on, and because I'm a hope-aholic, I know it will.

(Inspirational feminist music.)

[Image of protests today.]

(Blackout.)

END OF PART THREE

ACT TWO

TALKING CIRCLE

This takes place immediately after the conclusion of Act One, Part Three, without a break. It is not optional. It is the second act of the play.

ACTOR PLAYING GLORIA
Hi, I'm *[Name of actor]*. Welcome to Act Two.

FRANCESCA
Our Act Two will last about twenty minutes.

PATRENA
We are not taking an intermission. If you'd like to use the facilities, feel free to duck out and come back in.

JOANNA
This is not your traditional "theater talkback."

DELANNA

It's a talking circle. We will be learning from each other.

FEDNA

Talking circles are the energy cells of every movement. This is the way we discover (as Gloria says) —we're not crazy and we're not alone.

LIZ

Even if you don't speak, thank you for being present.

[Image of the organizing principles of Black Lives Matter:
Lead with Love
Low Ego
High Impact
Move at the Speed of Trust
—Alicia Garza, Patrisse Cullors and Opal Tometi:
The Movement for Black Lives Matter.]

PATRENA

(Referring to the guidelines) We'd like to share these guidelines with you for our discussion. Gloria says these are the best guidelines she's ever known—they were written by the three young black feminists who started the movement Black Lives Matter.

ACTOR PLAYING GLORIA

"Lead with love, low ego, high impact, and move at the speed of trust."

(If there is a guest for the performance, add:)

DELANNA

Tonight we have a special guest in our audience to help launch our talking circle: *[Guest name].*

(Fedna reads the bio of the special guest.

The cast signals to the seats in the audience, where the guest will be seated. Applause. The guest waves from their seat and/or stands up to acknowledge applause.)

ACTOR PLAYING GLORIA

(To the guest) So *[Guest name]*, we'd love you to launch our talking circle.

(If there is no special guest, start here:)

Can you tell us how or if the story we told tonight resonates with your story?

(The special guest, or first person to respond, speaks, and the talking circle develops. The actor playing Gloria leads, calling up people who want to speak. If there are microphones, a member of the ensemble brings a microphone to the person wanting to speak. After one of the ensemble says: "We have time for just one more story," and we hear it, the actor playing Gloria stands and ends with:)

We're going to end by making Gloria's organizer's deal with you: Promise that you will do at least one outrageous thing in the cause of social justice—beginning, say, at nine tomorrow morning. It can be as simple as saying:

JOANNA

Pick it up yourself!

ACTOR PLAYING GLORIA

Or as complicated as—

FEDNA

Deciding to run for political office.

ACTOR PLAYING GLORIA

Or as basic as—

LIZ

Telling each other our salaries—

DELANNA

Actually the one thing we know—

FRANCESCA

And when we share it, we discover what is and isn't fair.

PATRENA

If you do one outrageous thing in the next twenty-four hours,
I promise you two surefire results:

DELANNA

First, by the *next* day, the world will be better!

JOANNA

And second, you will have such a good time that you will never
again get up saying:

FEDNA

"*Will* I do an outrageous thing?" Only:

ACTOR PLAYING GLORIA

"*Which* outrageous thing will I do today?"
    Thank you for joining us.

(The actor playing Gloria and the ensemble exit.
    Music plays. It should be soft enough so that the audience can con-
verse as they leave.)

TIPS FOR THE TALKING CIRCLE

Keep the talking circle moving between audience members.

IF YOU GET STUCK

- Always ask the room: "Does anyone have the answer for that?" "Does anyone else feel that way?"
- Share your personal story.

IF SOMEONE GETS ANGRY

- Let another person in the audience speak—a lot of times the conflict resolves itself.

IF SOMEONE GOES ON TOO LONG

- Let them know that they have something of value to say, but other people in the space might have something of value to say.
- Thank them for sharing their story, but remind them that there are only twenty minutes for discussion, so other people must get a chance to share their story.
- If an ensemble member is holding the microphone, they can control the situation if it goes on too long.

ENSEMBLE CHARACTER BREAKDOWN

FEDNA

Smith College Student
SHOW Magazine Editor 2
Playboy Bunny 2
Plaza Hotel Fancy Guest
Oak Room Protester
Abortion Testifier 3
Party Guest
New York Magazine Colleague 2
Dorothy Pitman Hughes
Consciousness-Raising Group Woman of Color
Bra Burner
Founder 5
Woman Calling In
Ms. Magazine Receptionist
Coretta Scott King

Larry King
Friend 2
Planned Parenthood Representative
Women's March Participant

JOANNA

Smith College Student
Saul Bellow
Wardrobe Woman
Plaza Hotel Assistant Manager
Oak Room Protester 2
Party Guest
Gloria's Mother (Ruth)
Cab Driver
Consciousness-Raising Group Woman 3
Bra Burner
Founder 2
John Saywell
Letter Holder
Bella Abzug
Friend 1
Women's March Participant

PATRENA

Smith College Student
Bunny Mother
Playboy Nurse
Playboy Patron
New York Times Editor
Oak Room Protester 3
Dr. Sharpe
"Objective" Editor 2

Flo Kennedy
Consciousness-Raising Group Woman 2
Bra Burner
Truck Driver
African-American Woman—Minority Plank
Friend 4
Women's March Participant

DELANNA

Smith College Student
Gay Talese
SHOW Magazine Editor 3
Playboy Bunny
Playboy Doctor
The Woman on the Corner
Plaza Hotel Fancy Guest
Oak Room Protester 1
Abortion Testifier 1
Party Guest
1970s TV Reporter
Consciousness-Raising Group Woman 5
Bra Burner
Founder 1
Letter Writer 1
Native Woman—Minority Plank
Wilma Mankiller
2016 NBC Commentator

LIZ

Dean of Admissions
Bunny Trainer

Playboy Patron
Plaza Hotel Guest
Oak Room Maître d'
Party Guest
New York Magazine Colleague 1
"Objective" Editor 1
Man in Crowd
Consciousness-Raising Group Woman 6
Robin Morgan
CBC Voiceover
Woman in Crowd
Founder 4
Letter Writer 2
Jacob Javits
Friend 5
Gun Violence Interviewer
NBC Commentator
Women's March Participant

FRANCESCA

Smith College Student
SHOW Magazine Editor 1
Playboy Bunny 1
Plaza Hotel Guest
Press Agent
Oak Room Protester 4
Abortion Testifier 2
American Playwright
Speech Teacher
Consciousness-Raising Group Woman 1
Bra Burner
Founder 3
Letter Writer 3

Man on Phone
Woman of Color—Minority Plank
Asian/Pacific-American Woman—Minority Plank
Friend 3
America Ferrara

TIMELINE

1851 Sojourner Truth delivers her famous "Ain't I a Woman?" speech at the Women's Rights Convention

1920 The Nineteenth Amendment, granting women the right to vote, is ratified by Congress

1920s Gloria's mother Ruth (Nuneviller) Steinem, a journalist, is the first woman named the Sunday editor of the *Toledo Blade*

1934 Gloria Marie Steinem is born in Toledo, Ohio

1935-1945 Gloria travels nationwide with parents following her father's career as a traveling salesman

1947 Gloria's parents separate. Her mother suffers a "nervous breakdown," and Gloria cares for her ailing mother

1952 Gloria is admitted to Smith College

1956 Gloria graduates Phi Beta Kappa from Smith College with a bachelor's degree in Government

1957 Gloria has a secret abortion in London at the age of twenty-two; she will later speak publically about her abortion to assert the importance of "reproductive freedom" for women

1963 Gloria writes "A Bunny's Tale," an undercover exposé on the Playboy Club, which exposes the poor pay and working conditions for women there and brings her nationwide notoriety

1964 Bobby Kennedy runs for Senate from New York State

1965 Gloria meets with *New York Times* editor to deliver her Mary Lindsay interview

1968 Gloria is named a founding editor of *New York* Magazine and writes column "The City Politic" for the magazine

· Protest of *Miss America* Pageant in Atlantic City

1969 Gloria travels nationwide organizing events for the women's movement, freelance writing, and speaking on college campuses at engagements with Dorothy Pitman Hughes and Flo Kennedy

· Protest at The Plaza Hotel's Oak Room, which strictly enforces a "Men Only" lunch

· Gloria attends her first meeting held by a women's movement group addressing abortion; she is moved to begin writing and speaking out about feminism

· Gloria publishes the article "After Black Power, Women's Liberation" for *New York* Magazine; it brings her national fame as a feminist leader

· Gloria testifies about the Equal Rights Amendment before the United States Senate

1970 Abortion legalized in New York State

· Women's Strike for Equality

· Fiftieth Anniversary March of a Woman's Right to Vote

1971 Gloria co-founds *Ms.*, a magazine about second-wave feminist issues. Founding editors include Letty

Cottin Pogrebin, Mary Thom, Patricia Carbine, Joanne Edgar, Nina Finkelstein, and Mary Peacock

· Co-founds National Women's Political Caucus with Betty Friedan, Shirley Chisholm, Fannie Lou Hamer, Bella Abzug, and Mildred Jeffrey; the NWPC was created to increase "women's participation in all areas of political and public life"

1972 Gloria speaks at National Press Club

1973 *Roe v. Wade*

· Gloria co-founds the *Ms.* Foundation for women with Marlo Thomas and Letty Cottin Pogrebin

1977–1979 Works with Bella Abzug to establish the National Women's Conference

1981 Ruth Steinem dies

1984 Gloria's fiftieth birthday

1986 Gloria is diagnosed with breast cancer; successful treatment has allowed her to count herself among the survivors of the disease

1990 Gloria appears on *Larry King Live*

1992 Gloria's book *Revolution from Within: A Book of Self-Esteem* is published

1993 Gloria is inducted into the National Women's Hall of Fame

2000 At age sixty-six, she marries David Bale, despite a long-term opposition to marriage. The wedding is performed by the husband of Gloria's friend and mentor Wilma Mankiller, the first contemporary female Principle Chief of the Cherokee Nation

2003 David Bale dies of brain lymphoma

2011 The documentary *Gloria: In Her Own Words* airs on HBO

2013 Gloria is awarded the Presidential Medal of Freedom by President Barack Obama

2015 Gloria's memoir *My Life on the Road* is published

2016 Gloria delivers keynote speech at Planned Parenthood event in Memphis

2017 Gloria speaks at the Women's March on Washington

2018 The documentary play *Gloria: A Life* premieres Off-Broadway

2019 Gloria is currently the honorary co-chair of the Democratic Socialists of America and continues to travel and work internationally as an organizer and lecturer on the issues of equality

EMILY MANN is a Tony Award–winning Artistic Director and Resident Playwright in her thirtieth and final season at McCarter Theatre Center in Princeton, New Jersey. Her plays include: *Having Our Say*, adapted from the book by Sarah L. Delany and A. Elizabeth Delany with Amy Hill Hearth; *Execution of Justice*; *Still Life*; *Annulla, An Autobiography*; *Greensboro (A Requiem)*; *Meshugah*; *Mrs. Packard*; and *Hoodwinked (A Primer on Radical Islamism)*. Currently in development: *The Pianist*. Adaptations: *Baby Doll, Scenes from a Marriage, Uncle Vanya, The Cherry Orchard, The House of Bernarda Alba*, and *Antigone*. Awards include: Peabody, Hull-Warriner, NAACP, multiple Obies, Guggenheim Fellowship; Tony, Drama Desk, and Outer Critics Circle nominations; a Princeton University Honorary Doctorate of Arts, a Helen Merrill Playwright Award, and the Margo Jones Award. This year, she was awarded the TCG Visionary Leadership Award.